THE TRUTH ABOUT FORGIVENESS

MEGGAN LARSON

CONTENTS

PREFACE

What if I told you that you can be free? Free from the pain that comes with trauma, free from the grief that comes with loss, and free from the anger that comes with betrayal. What if there is a way for you to be truly at peace without receiving the apology you deserve, or without others changing their behavior? I'm here to tell you that it's not only possible, it's inevitable: when you forgive.

I spent a great portion of my life in bitterness. I was angry that I had been given away as a baby and then rejected again by my birth mother in adulthood. I was grieved that my innocence had been stolen by sexual abuse. I was full of shame over the way I had given myself over to guy after guy in search of someone to fill the gap I felt deep within my soul. I kept everyone at arm's length emotionally because I believed there was something intrinsically wrong with me. All of my experiential truth reinforced that belief, but little did I know I was stuck in a self-fulfilling prophecy cycle. I believed that something was wrong with me, then things would happen to confirm that belief, and I would then say: "See? I knew there was something wrong with me."

When my belief system changed, my life changed. When I changed what I focused on, my mind changed. When I changed how I spoke to myself, my words changed. Isn't that interesting? You can change your entire life by changing your mind, but it all starts with forgiveness.

THE TRUTH ABOUT FORGIVENESS

Learning to Forgive the Unforgivable

FORGIVENESS ~ WHAT IT ACTUALLY IS

*W*ebster's dictionary defines "to forgive" as *to cease to feel resentment against an offender, to give up claim to retaliation, and to grant relief from payment of (i.e. forgive a debt).*

Forgiving someone is letting yourself off the hook. Forgiving someone releases the emotions that tie you to that individual and allows you to move on in freedom and peace. When you forgive someone, you permit yourself to stop being triggered by things that remind you of that person. It's like letting out the breath you didn't know you were holding. It was slowly killing you, and you didn't even realize it. I love the saying, "Choosing not to forgive someone is like drinking poison and expecting it to hurt the other person." The truth is, it's not hurting them; it's hurting you. Let that sink in for a minute while I make my first point.

Unforgiveness is a joy-sucking vacuum. Have your negative feelings enriched your life or detracted from it? Have they given you extra time in your day or have they stolen precious minutes from your life? Have they made you a safe space for those around you or have they made you seem volatile? The best advice I can give is to be honest with yourself and take personal responsibility for where you're at. No one has the power to determine how you feel about something other than yourself.

THE SECOND POINT I want to develop about forgiveness is that it's a choice. Many believe that forgiveness is a feeling, but that's simply not true. If you wait to feel like you're ready to forgive, you may wait for an eternity. The beauty of our feelings is that they follow our will and not the other way around. I know this can feel opposite to where your experiential truth has led you, but hear me out. We have the power to create our own realities within the framework of our thoughts and words. If you don't believe me, study quantum physics. Every single time someone hurts me I say these words out loud:

"I choose to forgive (insert name here) with my will. I pray that my feelings follow quickly."

This has worked for me nearly every single time because I now know the truth of the power of my will. It is truly a freeing reality to realize that we don't have to be tossed around by our feelings like a tree swaying in the breeze. Let me illustrate this with the following experience a client of mine had.

CALLIE THOUGHT she was in love with Jason. Even though she was in a committed relationship, she had bumped into someone from her past a couple of months earlier, and since then they'd been inseparable. They talked, they texted, they emailed, they did video chats. You name it, they did it. They woke up talking to each other first thing and went to bed saying good-night to each other last. It was intense and passionate, and Callie was strongly considering leaving her partner for Jason.

It didn't start that way of course. In the beginning, Callie was upfront about her relationship and told Jason they could only ever be friends. He quickly agreed, telling her he just wanted them to be in each other's lives no matter how. The more they talked, the more frustrated he seemed to become. He would remark on how hard it was becoming for him not to say what he wanted to. He even told her he loved her at one point, which confused her deeply. When she pressed him, he told her he just meant it as a friend would say it, but she knew he meant more. He started sending her messages of an intimate nature, and though she knew she should walk away, the pull was too strong for Callie. She deleted the more intimate messages just in case Alex came upon them, guarded her phone at all times, and panicked whenever a text came in when she was with her husband.

She could think of nothing but Jason, and even though she deeply loved Alex, he was starting to get on her nerves. Everything from the way he chewed to the way he smiled was ticking her off, and the more she thought about it, the more she wondered what she had ever even seen in him. They had been fighting more and more before she bumped into Jason, and she thought maybe it was meant to be. She pulled away from Alex emotionally and physically, convincing herself that she should always have been with Jason. She had known him first, and they had dated in high school. Jason hadn't been ready to commit to anyone at that time, and frankly, neither had Callie — yet things were different now. Jason told her how he thought he must have been in love with her back then but that it had scared him, so he'd run. Callie thought of nothing but spending time with Jason. In the back of her mind, she felt bad about what that would mean for Alex since he had always been so good to her. He was really the first man she had ever let herself love. But this was different. This was passionate and exciting, and she was sure Jason loved her too. He wouldn't admit that it was more than friendship, but how could it not be? He talked to her all day long, sent messages that made her blush, and told her how important she was to him.

Finally, after weeks and weeks of this, she told Jason how confused she was and how she thought that maybe she should be with him instead of Alex. To her shock and disbelief, Jason told her that he wasn't in love with her. He admitted to having strong feelings, but that he couldn't tell her what she wanted to hear. He told her he loved her but wasn't "in love," with her and that even if she were single, he wasn't sure he was ready to be with her. Callie felt utterly stupid. How could she have convinced herself that Jason was in love with her when he had told her it was just friendship? She was furious with him, but mostly she was angry with herself. She had nearly thrown away her relationship to an absolutely wonderful man, for some childish guy who saw her as a challenge instead of someone worth his devotion. Worse, she knew she had to tell Alex what had happened and pray that he would forgive her.

Much to her surprise, Alex did forgive her, and quickly! He told her that he was in the marriage for the long haul and that though what she had done hurt him deeply, he was sorry for giving her a reason to stray. She couldn't believe it. She knew she didn't deserve such a wonderful and forgiving man. She became even angrier with Jason for almost ruining what was obviously the love of her life. She didn't want to forgive him, especially when he wasn't even sorry. He continued to call and text as though nothing had happened. She eventually told him to stop contacting her when the stress of the situation caused her to develop an ulcer.

Months passed and she found herself still angry. She couldn't think of Jason without a sudden pain in her chest and a fury that scared her. How dare he play with her heart and emotions like that? She wished he had just left her alone and never come into her life, to begin with. She began to realize that although he was no longer in her life, she was still dealing with the aftermath. The ulcer was getting worse, she had begun to gain weight rapidly, and her hair had even started falling out. She still wasn't ready to forgive him, but she knew she needed to. He would probably never understand the pain and confusion he had caused her, but if she wanted to stop gaining weight and losing her hair then she needed to let it go. She chose to forgive him with her will and prayed that her feelings would follow.

It took a few times, but eventually her feelings did follow, and she was no longer bonded to him through rage. She understood that he was just a broken man who needed Jesus, and that she needed to stay far away from him. She has stopped gaining weight, her ulcer is healing, and her hair looks great again. She won't soon forget the pain she caused, and she had to spend time forgiving herself as well, but she uses it as a lesson on how to protect herself emotionally. The next time an "old friend" tried to get inappropriate with her, she immediately shut it down and hasn't heard back since.

Forgiveness is like a balm to a nasty infection. It soothes, heals, and protects. You may have every reason to withhold forgiveness from someone, but the longer you do, the worse it will be — for you. Callie's lack of forgiveness didn't affect Jason at all. He probably still doesn't even understand his wrongdoing. But for Callie to truly heal and move on, she needed to forgive, even if she didn't feel like it. Feeling ready is not a precursor to forgiveness. Forgiveness is a choice and an action. Feelings actually have nothing to do with it at all.

FORGIVENESS ~ WHAT IT ISN'T

*N*ow that we know what forgiveness is, let me explain what it isn't since that is just as important. Just because you've forgiven someone, that doesn't mean you need to barbecue with them. When someone wounds you deeply, it's important and permissible to set boundaries, especially if this kind of hurt has taken place before. We are human; we don't just forgive and forget when the wound is deep. We're allowed to take a step back from the relationship or even end it altogether. That doesn't mean you aren't in forgiveness; it simply means that you need some space to heal, and that's okay. Forgiving someone doesn't mean that you have to let them have an all-access pass to your life, especially if they are not repentant. As a Christian, this is something I struggled with greatly. After all, doesn't turning the other cheek mean to completely forgive and forget? If you're struggling with that too, here are a couple of verses that should help settle this in your spirit:

"Get rid of all bitterness, rage, and anger, brawling and slander, along with every form of malice. Be kind and compassionate to one another, forgiving each other, just as in Christ God forgave you." Ephesians 4:31-32

"If your brother or sister sins, go and point out their fault, just between the two of you. If they listen to you, you have won them over. But if they will not listen, take one or two others along, so that 'every matter may be established by the testimony of two or three witnesses.' If they still refuse to listen, tell it to the church; and if they refuse to listen even to the church, treat them as you would a pagan or a tax collector." Matthew 18:15-18

Again, let me illustrate this with a story (please be aware that the following story is about sexual abuse and may be a trigger for some people):

JENNY COULD STILL FEEL his hands on her and smell his wretched breath on her face. She was six, and he was a relative she should have been able to trust. They were all wrong. Standing outside of her grandparents' home playing in the front yard, her uncle pulled her close, stuck his hand down her bathing suit bottom, and started rubbing her privates. She tried to pull away, but he just held her tighter whispering, "Shhhhh, it's okay, it's okay". But it wasn't okay, and she knew it.

Eventually, she was able to yank free from him and run inside, but she didn't tell anyone. Maybe it was because she didn't think anyone would believe her. Nevertheless, the rest of that trip was spent awkwardly ensuring she was never alone with him and being terrified to go to sleep. From the moment she was first violated, she changed. She was forever robbed of her innocence because, for the first time, she felt unsafe. For the first time, she was painfully aware that not only were there dangerous people in the world, but her parents weren't able to protect her from them. That single violation shaped the course of her future, leading to further violations from different people and causing her to feel as though her body were not her own. She was often touched in private places by her friends' brothers or cousins, and she just closed her eyes as tightly as she could and pretended she was somewhere else while it happened.

As she grew older, she experimented with her friends at sleepovers, thinking it was perfectly normal. She even pushed some of her friends to do things they weren't comfortable with, much to her deep shame and regret. She and her best friend stumbled onto pornography before she was a teenager, and she continued to watch it regularly. Years later, when Jenny finally worked up the courage to confide in her mother about what had happened with her uncle that day, her mother chose not to believe her. It was like a slap in the face. It reinforced the shame she felt and the false belief that she should never tell anyone when those things happened. She buried the pain, the fear, and the shame deep down within herself and carried on as a fragmented version of who she should have been.

Jenny lost her virginity at the age of fifteen, seeing it as something that she needed to get rid of instead of something sacred and special to save. She gave herself to any guy who showed interest because she felt unlovable, unworthy, and disgusting all the time. Sex was not something she particularly enjoyed; it was just the natural consequence of getting close to a guy. It wasn't until she was in her twenties and slept with a friend from work simply because he liked her better than her roommate that she considered herself to have hit rock bottom.

Her older sister had come to know Jesus a few years before and walked her through giving her heart to the Lord. She was a new creation, but she still felt dirty. It wasn't until she forgave her uncle for violating her and forgave her parents for not protecting her that she was finally able to shed the shame and guilt and walk in freedom. Did her uncle deserve to be forgiven? No. Molesting a child is not something that deserves forgiveness. Robbing a child of innocence is cruel and horrifying. Her parents should have protected her; they should have been watching her that day instead of letting her play by herself. So many things should have happened to protect that little girl, but they didn't.

. . .

JUST BECAUSE SOMEONE doesn't deserve to be forgiven doesn't mean that you shouldn't forgive them. Please hear me on this. The reason I feel this way is because Jesus forgave me for every single thing I've ever done, am currently doing, or will ever do. He's forgiven me for every awful thought I've ever had or will ever have. I am not in a position to withhold forgiveness no matter what the person has done. The main reason this is so important is that forgiveness is not for them; it's for me and it's for you! If you don't know Jesus, then simply consider this: Holding on to that much hatred and anger is damaging to your body. Did you know that anger and hatred are stored in the liver? What do you think that's doing to your liver when you insist on holding onto those negative emotions? Diseases are born out of unforgiveness.

You have every right to be angry with the person who violated you, but the best "revenge" you could ever get is to forgive them, move on, and live your life in happiness. Reporting them to the police is also a wise thing to do. To be clear, just because you've forgiven someone doesn't mean they shouldn't be held accountable for their actions. If someone has done something to you that is against the law, they should be prosecuted. I know that they don't deserve to be forgiven. But don't you deserve to be free? Jesus came so that we would have life and have it abundantly. Living as a shell of who you were meant to be is not how your story should end. Forgive, sweet friend, and let Jesus heal the parts of your heart that need to be healed, or at least free yourself from the negativity.

WHAT IF THEY HAVEN'T APOLOGIZED?

*T*his can be a tough one, can't it? It feels wrong to extend forgiveness to someone who isn't even apologetic for what they've done. Shouldn't they at least have to apologize for me to forgive them? In a nutshell, no. Trust me, this is a good thing! If forgiveness were dependent on someone's apology, then we'd all be in trouble. Some people just aren't sorry. Others don't even realize that an apology is being expected. Should your freedom rely on the actions of someone else? I want to share an especially painful chapter of my history with you to (hopefully) encourage you. Here goes:

IT. Was. Brutal. Being rejected by anyone at any time is a pretty bitter pill to swallow. But being rejected (AGAIN) by your biological mother? That is a different level of pain altogether.

I had always known that I was adopted. My parents often told me the story of my adoption as a child, usually in the form of a bedtime story. I knew the story well. My mom had wanted a fourth child, but no way would she go through another pregnancy. She already had two boys and a girl, and she wanted another girl. There was only one way to guarantee that outcome. Meanwhile, I had been placed into the foster care system to await a family; only, they had placed me with a foster mother who had just experienced a devastating loss. For two years she had taken care of a child from birth, and the child had just been rehomed. She had wanted that child so desperately and had grown to love her as her own. Unfortunately, she was not allowed to keep the baby; and almost as quickly as they removed that child from her home, they replaced her with me. This time she wouldn't make the same mistake. She would keep her distance emotionally and ensure that she didn't grow attached to me. I felt it. Even as a baby, I felt it. My chart said that I cried constantly and was basically inconsolable. They thought something might be wrong with me.

The agency called my adoptive parents, who drove for several hours to come and meet this colicky baby, and as soon as I was in their arms, I stopped crying. It's like I knew they were safe. That basically sealed the deal, and I went home with them shortly after. This was how the story always went, and as a child, I ate it up. My mom kept in touch with my birth mother through letters and pictures, and when I was old enough I started writing my own letters to her once in a while. We met when I was a boy-crazy fourteen-year-old, and I think the reins were officially passed off to me at that point. If I wanted to continue a relationship with my birth mother, my mom wasn't going to do it for me anymore. It was mostly fine. I'd go see her maybe once a year, sometimes more. We'd hang out with her kids; I'd go cry in the bathroom for reasons unknown to me, and we'd stay in touch through emails. It wasn't really until we were seen in public by one of her coworkers that I had the epiphany.

Her co-worker came to our table, looked back and forth between us, and bluntly asked who I was (since I looked almost exactly like her). Instead of introducing me, she said I was no one and that she'd explain later. Ouch. I was still a secret. It turned out no one, aside from a few key family members, knew about me, and that was not going to change. It didn't bother me at first, but then we'd watch old family videos together, and her and my grandparents would all laugh about the fact that she was only shot from the neck up the year of my birth. And once we were at my biological family's barbecue and they realized one of their aunts didn't know who I was, and they thought it was hilarious. They didn't introduce me.

The last straw for me was when my great-grandmother died, and I asked to attend the funeral. I was now thirty-two years old, and had been in my birth mother's life for a solid eighteen years. She told me that I could attend, but that many people wouldn't know who I was, and I must not explain. I was to introduce myself as a friend of the family. I wasn't upset that they weren't going to make a big announcement about who I was at the funeral; I obviously understood it was not the time or place. What did upset me was that I was still a secret after all that time. There shouldn't have been a need to introduce me. I had started having my own children by then, and the thought of them feeling like dirty little secrets was overwhelming. I knew I couldn't let it go on any further, and so I wrote a letter.

I explained how I felt, how hard it was for me to feel that way after so many years, and that I could not and would not let my children be treated that way. I knew she wouldn't fawn over them on social media because no one knew she was a grandmother, yet I wondered what would happen when one of my half-sisters had a baby. Would they be introduced as her first grandchild? It cut me up inside. In the letter, I asked that we either continue our relationship out in the open or that we didn't continue it at all. I couldn't take it anymore, and I still believe that no human being should ever be kept a secret.

To my shock and dismay, I received a letter in return telling me she had no intention of ever telling people who I was. I was also accused of being a religious zealot who was trying to worm my way into her family. She was confused as to why I was trying to be a part of their family when I had my own.

I can hardly explain to you the depth of pain that caused me. I read the letter once, closed it, and never opened it again. It shattered a big chunk of my heart, and I felt completely numb. I think I stayed in my bed for hours that day, just staring at the wall. She chose her secret over a relationship with me and her grandchildren. Her secret was more important than any of us.

SUFFICE IT TO SAY, she has never apologized for what was probably the most painful moment of my entire life. And I don't know that she ever will. And you know what? I'm okay with that. Crazy, right? Here's the thing: My forgiveness can't depend on her apology. What if it never comes? Am I going to stay bitter, angry, and resentful, forever awaiting an apology that isn't coming? My feelings do not affect her, good or bad. By staying in a negative frame of mind and constantly replaying the hurt over and over in my head and heart, I am punishing myself. Haven't I been robbed of enough? Haven't you?

I DON'T KNOW what hurts have befallen you, and I won't pretend that it doesn't matter. It does matter. It matters more than we could even know. But in this life, we get to choose how to respond to devastating circumstances. We get to decide whether we are going to wallow in even well-deserved self-pity, or whether we're going to pick ourselves back up, dust ourselves off, and carry on. Holding onto unforgiveness doesn't hurt the person we're angry with. It hurts us! We deserve better than what's happened to us; that's a fact. But hear me on this: They probably don't even understand the depth of pain they've caused. And if they do, maybe they don't care. Everyone has a story, and everyone has been deeply wounded by someone. That's the way it goes, isn't it? We've all heard the saying: "Hurt people hurt other people". Do you want to be stuck in a cycle of anger and hurt? If you don't lay this burden down, it's going to wind up hurting others, whether you mean to or not.

I can't imagine the pain and embarrassment my birth mother has gone through. I would not have traded places with her in a million years. But all that pain doesn't excuse the pain it's caused me. It does help me understand it a bit better and even have some sympathy for her. And I could never have come to that thought process without first letting go and choosing to forgive her.

Until you let go, really let go, of how badly someone has wounded you, you won't heal. Time doesn't heal everything. I would even go so far as to say time doesn't heal *anything*. All it does is cover the wound with a scab, making it feel a bit better but never fully closing. Any time you think about the offense, the scab gets ripped off, exposing the pain again and again. Forgiveness heals. Time just delays the process if it isn't actually dealt with. Ask yourself whether it's time for you to be free of the pain this has been causing you. Only you can decide.

WHAT EFFECT DOES
UNFORGIVENESS REALLY HAVE
ON THE BODY?

I've been studying the effect of unforgiveness on the body for over a decade. It all started when a friend of mine was raving about a book that a pastor/doctor had written about the correlation between disease and unforgiveness. She was giving me examples from the book and said something like, "Did you know a lump in your breast can actually be caused by bitterness towards your mother or mother-in-law?" I stared at her for a few seconds and then excused myself. She didn't know this, but I had actually found a lump in one of my breasts the week before, AND I had been extremely angry towards my mother-in-law over a situation that had destroyed my husband's relationship with a lot of his family and two close friends. I immediately spent time forgiving her and releasing my anger, and within twenty-four hours the lump had disappeared. I'm not a doctor, and this should not be taken as medical advice. All I'm saying is that after this experience I began looking into the correlation between negative emotions and our body systems because that really caught my attention.

One of my favorite resources is the app "Feelings Buried Alive Never Die" (it's also a book by Karol Truman). Whenever I'm working with a client and they are experiencing discomfort in the same area again and again, I look up the body part in the app just to see if what it says resonates with them. For example, when someone keeps complaining about their ankle hurting, I'll pull up the app and read it to them: "Fears falling or failing, inflexibility, instability in the present situation, feeling overworked but can't quit, feels there is no relief from pressures of life." I'll ask if any of that resonates with the person, and if so, it just gives them something to consider exploring.

I HAD a job once that started wonderfully, but over time the commitment became so great that I was suffocating under the weight of it. I felt like I was on call 24/7, and the work was taking a good forty to sixty hours per week for which I was getting paid about $3.50 an hour, when it was all said and done. I didn't want to leave my boss hanging by quitting because she really depended on me, but at the same time I knew I needed to quit because my kids had stopped asking me to read to them since I was always too busy. My heart was broken, and I felt torn. A few weeks before I quit, my ankle started hurting; a lot. It got to the point where I was limping up and down the stairs and could hardly walk, even though nothing had actually happened to injure it. When I looked at what the feelings app said, I instantly knew what was going on: *"Feeling overworked but can't quit."* Still, I wrestled with the decision because I really dislike letting people down. Once I decided to quit, my ankle went back to normal, and it was a lesson for me not to ignore the physical symptoms that could be due to an emotional trigger.

Injury and disease do not necessarily have a deeper meaning, but I will say that it catches my attention whenever something physical is happening to me. It's a good habit to get into, to explore the emotional root of a physical problem. So how does this relate to unforgiveness? Simple. When you are stuck in unforgiveness that's when negative feelings begin to fester. They grow like cancer deep within your body, and physical issues can start to manifest themselves. Grief is stored in the lungs, anger is stored in the liver, frustration is stored in the back, etc. I think you get my drift. Feelings don't just disappear from the body, they get stored. When you forgive, you're able to release yourself from carrying those negative emotions and they, therefore, don't have a chance to wreak havoc on your body.

Do you see why forgiveness is mostly beneficial to you? I mean, of course it feels nice when someone we've hurt forgives us, but the benefits are so much greater to us when we're the ones releasing the anger, bitterness, and grief. Not only does it feel great on an emotional level, but it also saves us from potential physical ramifications as well.

HOW DO I ACTUALLY FORGIVE SOMEONE?

The first step to forgiveness is pretty simple. You have to *choose* to forgive. Your feelings follow your will, so you need to decide to do this. Say it out loud because it makes it more real. Speaking forgiveness out loud interrupts all your thoughts screaming at you not to. Even if you have to say it through clenched teeth, do it anyway. And finally, whenever your feelings start to rear their ugly head and tell you that you haven't forgiven, remind them that they follow your will, and since you chose to forgive, it's a done deal.

The second step to forgiveness, one I do immediately afterward, is to pray. I pray and I ask Jesus to help my feelings follow quickly. You see, just because you've made the choice to forgive someone doesn't mean that your feelings are going to match that right away. You're still going to have all the angry/hurt/sad feelings, and that's to be expected. I find that when I ask for help with my feelings, Jesus comes through every single time. If you don't know Jesus yet, then you do what's comfortable for you.

Of course, there are times I need to repeat this process if the trauma is particularly painful, but it's been a very effective way of helping me get to the good part of forgiveness: the part when you don't feel so betrayed anymore, and the part when you can finally begin to let go. Let me illustrate.

RECENTLY I WAS HAVING a heart to heart with a dear friend, and something came up that threw me for a loop.

Someone had lied about me. I mean, full-on made something up that painted me in a horrible light, and I was shocked. Disbelief filled me, and then dread took over as I wondered to myself who else this person had told this story to. Who else honestly believed that I would actually do that to someone, let alone someone I cared about? Plus, I considered this person like family.

I *almost* let myself get angry. This was unjust! This was unfair! This was total manipulation! I could feel it bubbling up inside me even right there on the phone. I wanted to scream out like I was in a court of law, "I OBJECT!"

But feelings are a choice, and I chose long ago not to be led by them any longer. I had to decide at that moment if I was going to give up precious mind space to this situation, or if I was just going to forgive, let it go, and move on. I chose to forgive, and I know that it was effective because by the next day I had completely forgotten about it.

Occasionally I'll get a pang of sadness because being betrayed hurts. It's not pleasant when someone lies about you and you can't even defend yourself. It's not fun when someone you trusted stabs you in the heart. I'd say back, but it's really the heart, isn't it? It's shocking when someone you thought you knew acts in such a way that you realize you never really knew this person at all.

All I can do is let my character speak for itself. I'm not going to track down everyone this lie was probably told to and clear up the truth. If they believe something like that about me so easily, then that's not on me. I know who I am, I know how I treat people, and anyone who knows me even a little should know that I would never do what I was accused of doing.

The beauty of forgiveness is that I don't have to let it eat me up inside. I don't have to let it occupy my mind and prey on my emotions. I can just give it up to Jesus, let it go, pray for that person (my choice, you might not be there yet, and that's okay), and move the heck on, living my best life. That's the choice I'll make every single time.

WHAT ABOUT WHEN THE BETRAYAL HAPPENED SO LONG AGO?

*T*here are times we can falsely believe that what happened in the past stays in the past. Sadly, that's just not the case. Just because something happened to you years ago, doesn't mean that it's not still affecting you. When I'm working through Aroma Freedom Technique, I gently guide clients through a process that identifies what's been stopping them from moving forward in life. The way it makes them feel brings up memories that sometimes have nothing to do with the goal they're currently trying to achieve. This happens because the experience they had in the past was so impactful (or traumatizing) that it caused their brain and body to protect them from feeling that way in the future.

WHEN I WAS ten years old, I attended a summer camp at a new school. The very first day I became friends with a few girls; most of them were white and another was black. I was thrilled to make new friends on my first day, and I remember going back the next day full of excitement. I ran up to my group of friends and failed to notice the changed vibe. The leader of the group turned to me and said: "We've decided that we can only have one black girl in our group."

I stood there confused; I didn't understand. I was half black, and I lived with a white family. Surely, she wasn't talking about me. She went on ...

"We chose her."

She pointed to the other black girl, who was looking down at the ground, and then they all turned their backs on me and kept talking amongst themselves. I walked away slowly, shrugged as though it didn't bother me, and swallowed it all down because, at the time, the only way to process that kind of pain was simply not to. I didn't make other friends at that camp, and, frankly struggled to make any friends at all from that point on.

The memory of that experience came up recently during a powerful session, and I sobbed for that little girl whose heart was shattered. My daughter is the same age I was then, and that fact broke me even more because I couldn't imagine her going through something so awful simply because of the color of her skin. I also looked back at the pattern of my friendships and realized that I shied away from groups. I only made friends with individuals, never with groups of people. My experiential truth had taught me that groups of girls were unsafe, and I, therefore, should avoid them. I knew that I needed to forgive those girls for treating my ten-year-old self so cruelly, and once I did, I stopped being fearful of making friends with groups of women.

Dealing with the hurts we've experienced, the trauma we've endured, and releasing those who have caused us the most anguish will set us free from the trap of fear and cycles of brokenness. Even though that pain had happened more than twenty years earlier, it was still affecting my daily life. I can't know how many friendships I missed out on because of that pattern of fear, but I do know it's not going to happen anymore because I chose to forgive.

Now, whenever I see someone behaving horrifically to someone else, I wonder to myself what could have happened in this person's life to make him or her treat another human being this way? What horrors has this person endured to think that this behaviour is acceptable? Maybe it's a naive way of looking at things, but when you work with people in the capacity that I do, one thing becomes crystal clear: Everyone is hurting. Everyone has gone through terrible experiences that are buried deep down within them. Unless forgiveness is released, they are bound to repeat patterns that don't serve them to avoid future pain. The sad truth is that they're also avoiding future happiness by staying stuck in those destructive patterns.

WHEN YOU CAN'T GET AWAY
FROM THE PERSON WHO KEEPS
HURTING YOU

*W*hen someone in your life is constantly hurting you, it can be extremely difficult to forgive over and over again. When they are unrepentant about it, it's even worse. If at all possible, it's important to set boundaries and get some distance or even end the relationship. When that isn't possible, staying in a constant state of forgiveness is important. What I mean by that is to forgive every day. Chances are this person is a thorn in your side, and as awful as this is to suggest, they may get some pleasure from making your life miserable. I've had such "friendships" in my life, and one such friendship caused me so much stress that I honestly believe it was one of the main contributing factors to my being diagnosed with cancer back in 2012. Constant stress for five years? Yep, that'll do it.

When the person causing you this kind of hardship is not someone that you can just cut out of your life, then it's necessary to create and stick to firm boundaries. If you're living with the person, then perhaps some space is needed, as well as some professional mediation or therapy. If this person is not living with you, then they don't need access to your life 24/7. If they won't stop texting you, block their number. Did you know you can block and unblock someone's number regularly? Maybe you can have hours of operation for them. Tell them your new boundaries and let them know when they're pushing.

It can be incredibly difficult to create and stick to boundaries when you have let others walk all over you for most of your life. I'm living proof that it's possible to stand firm in your boundaries even if you never used to. It also gets easier to do the more you exercise this muscle. No one will actually die if you don't respond to a text or a social-media message immediately. Do it on your own terms or not at all. Author Lysa Terkeurst says it beautifully in her book *Forgiving What You Can't Forget*: "Boundaries aren't to push others away. Boundaries are to help hold me together." I also saw an amazing picture from recording artist Toby Mac that states: "Toxic people will try to make you think you're holding a grudge. Nah, that's a boundary."

There is absolutely nothing wrong with boundaries, and the only people who seem to have issues with them are the ones who benefitted the most from you not having any. It's a real shock to them when you throw some up, but it's the healthiest thing you can do.

Without boundaries, you'll get burnt out so badly that you might pull away from everyone to protect yourself. That doesn't serve you, and if you're not careful you'll end up pushing away the good relationships too. Set your boundaries and stick to them so that you don't fall into bitterness. You determine how people treat you, so make sure to severely limit the access that toxic people have to you. At the end of the day, you don't owe them a thing.

THE MANY LAYERS OF
FORGIVENESS

*F*orgiveness can sometimes be an evolving process. The reason for that is that at times you aren't aware of everything a person might have done to you, and as more truth comes to light, more forgiveness is needed. I went through this recently, and it was a huge epiphany that I'll share with you (though it is, of course, through my perspective alone because it's the only one I have).

Do you remember the ankle story I mentioned earlier? When I knew I had to quit my job? Well, there's more to that story. For thirteen years, I had been friends with the person I worked for. Over the course of our working together, we became like family to each other, or so I thought. Quitting that job was one of the hardest things I've ever had to do because I cared so much about this person, and I didn't want to let her down. We had big plans, and we were creating an empire together. I had stayed with her for five years while everyone else left. She wasn't paying me much, but it's what she could afford; and I knew that when things really took off, I would be well compensated, according to her promises.

The problem came when I made a new friend. I began following her directions for my own business, and things were really starting to go well for me. I was absolutely thrilled that after five years of struggling I was finally seeing tangible results. My boss told me that she could no longer promote me (for reasons I'll keep to myself), and at that moment I realized that we had never been building an empire together; I had been building hers and hers alone. This was a painful revelation to me, but I had done it to myself. After seeking wise counsel, I decided that it was time for me to step out from under her shadow and shine in the way I was meant to shine. I naively thought she would be happy for me. We were practically family, after all. It turns out that was a one-way feeling, and we basically haven't spoken since. We went from speaking all day, every day to nothing at all. It hurt so much, and I have cried many tears over it.

Eventually, I picked myself up off the ground and really began to flourish. I was serving authentically from my heart and actually making money while doing it. It was amazing and thrilling, and I rose in my success very quickly. I was creating courses, and they were selling like crazy. I was even customizing people's websites for them and charging $75/hour when I had been making peanuts before. Then, people started asking for advice. At first, I was fine with it; I'm a helper, after all. But after a while, I started to feel bitter about it. They were asking me to spell out everything I was doing to create success, and I felt myself responding like Gollum in *The Lord Of The Rings*. I wondered what the heck was going on with me. Those were ugly feelings that I didn't like seeing pop up. I had a Facetime coffee date with a close friend who has a beautiful gift of nailing exactly what's going on, and she asked me a very pointed question.

"Meggan, do you think you're feeling this way because you are beginning to see your true value and realizing how much your former friend stole of your time, your finances, and your emotions?"

Ouch. I was still angry. I thought I had forgiven her already, and the truth is I had. But as I grew as a person, I uncovered more reasons why I needed to forgive again. When I first quit, I didn't realize that I could have been charging so much more for what I was doing. I didn't realize that having me on call basically 24/7 wasn't a healthy thing. I didn't realize that I would be discarded once I was no longer useful to her. This was another layer of pain that I needed to deal with, and it caught me by surprise.

A sweet friend of mine likes to say that anger is your power returning, and that really resonated with me. I was furious the more I thought about what had transpired during and after working for her, but I also didn't want to stay stuck in that anger. The reason I was feeling so bitter towards people who were trying to take from me (so it seemed, I don't really believe they were) was that I had been robbed for so long, and this was my way of standing up and saying "no." It wasn't their fault that their questions were triggering me. They couldn't have known how deeply hurt I had been. I needed to forgive again, and so this time I wrote a letter. I furiously scribbled out everything I wanted to say to her, and by the end I found myself wishing her well and hoping that someday she'd see the light. I threw that letter into my fireplace and watched it burn as tears streamed down my face. It was a healing exercise, and I knew that I had reached another level of forgiveness — which brings me to my next point.

You've got to let yourself feel to heal.

I used to live in a constant state of numbness. Whenever I got really hurt by someone (emotionally), I would just shut down to the point where I could no longer feel anything. I honestly thought it served me well. The truth is, I was just adding more layers of pain to work through later on. Does that sound familiar? When you've been wounded by someone, it's actually a form of trauma. Trauma is defined as "a deeply distressing or disturbing experience." When someone betrays you, assaults you, lies about you or to you, these are all forms of trauma. The problem comes when we: a) don't identify it correctly, so we falsely believe we should just get over it; and b) when we push the feelings down instead of dealing with them.

I was someone who rarely cried. Any time I would sense those pricks behind my eyes, I would immediately shut them down. I got so good at it that I was able to stop tears in their tracks every single time. What I didn't realize, though, is that tears are healing. Tears are releasing the pent-up emotions within yourself. Tears are a *good* thing! It's important to let yourself feel your feelings to heal through them.

If the thought of letting yourself feel the pain is terrifying, you're in good company. If you truly want to be free from the chains of trauma, though, it's important to begin processing what you're feeling deep down inside. That can look like writing a letter you never intend to send or letting yourself cry or letting yourself scream the rage out. Whatever that looks like for you is okay (unless it's hurting yourself or someone else of course). You deserve to be free of the feelings that you've been repressing for far too long. You already know what can happen to the feelings you stuff down. Why put yourself through that?

Feeling your feelings is a lot like throwing up. The buildup is awful, the release is terrible, but you feel so much better afterward don't you? Forgiveness has layers, friend. It's okay to feel what you feel; just don't stay stuck there.

HOW DO YOU KNOW WHEN YOU'VE TRULY FORGIVEN SOMEONE?

*I*t can be challenging to know when you are truly free from the burden of holding onto unforgiveness. It's not always a quick release into peaceful oblivion. In fact, it's rarely like that from my experience. What it *is* like is gradually realizing you no longer feel angry or hurt or sad when you think about that person. It's truly wishing them well even if you don't necessarily want to hang out with them. It's noticing the things that used to trigger you before don't anymore. That's also how you can tell if you haven't completely forgiven someone yet. How you react to something is just an indication of what's going on internally. It's not right or wrong; it just is what it is. Use it as a way of identifying where you're at and moving through it.

. . .

I HAD a horrid misunderstanding with a friend once. We went from hanging out several times a week, spending Friday nights together as families and always inviting each other to birthdays and activities to absolutely nothing. We became fast friends, and it ended almost as quickly. It was one of the most painful things I have ever gone through. Part of the problem was that we still had to see each other weekly, and it was so hard to pretend like things were fine when they weren't. I really don't do "fake" well.

The other part of the problem is that I admitted my fault in the misunderstanding and apologized profusely. Instead of doing the same, my friend shifted the blame over to me entirely, and I was shamed for setting boundaries. For three years I grieved this friendship while keeping up the pretense that everything was fine. We sent funny memes back and forth now and then, but we didn't get together. It was like the slowest most painful breakup ever. Eventually, I found my voice and put a stop to the charade. I sought wise counsel (literally from a mediation counselor who had helped my sister and me through a painful spot in our relationship ~ thanks again, Ruth!) and she and another dear friend prayerfully walked me through everything. They assured me that I wasn't crazy, that this was in fact an unhealthy relationship, and that it was okay to go our separate ways.

I truly wish nothing but absolute peace and happiness to this former friend. I'm sure I would be glad to run into her on the street. That's how I know I've truly forgiven her. The pain, the longing, the sadness are all gone. Instead, there's just a fondness for what was and the hope that maybe someday we'll be friends again; but if not, that's okay too.

WHEN YOU ARE TRIGGERED and instantly react, it's important to take note of that reaction and understand that it's simply a picture of what's going on inside. Our reactions are very telling. Following up with honest questions like, "Hmm, why did I respond that way?" or, "Gee, that seems like an overreaction. What's really going on here?" will lead us to the truth. When you realize that your reactions are less and less strong, that your feelings towards the person are either neutral or even positive, and that you aren't triggered by thinking about them or when someone mentions them, congratulations: You're in forgiveness.

SOMETIMES IT TAKES A FEW TRIES, so don't lose hope if you still find yourself angry after choosing to forgive someone. That doesn't mean you didn't do it properly; your emotions may just need some additional time to calm down. Let that be okay and just let yourself feel what you feel. I also find that going through big emotions can mean that you're not taking deep breaths. Just the act of taking a big deep breath through whatever emotion you're experiencing intensely will help calm you down. I've done it through burning rage and wracking sobs with amazing results. I was able to refocus and let go just by breathing through it.

HOW TO PROTECT YOURSELF FROM OTHER PEOPLE'S NEGATIVITY

I don't like to throw the word "toxic" around as I honestly believe that people only act the way they do because they've been hurt. I guess I don't believe that people are inherently "toxic," but sometimes that person is toxic for *you*. I have many family members that I would consider toxic for me. I don't believe they are evil people by any means; however, their words and actions often result in my feeling shamed, put down or worse. I choose not to surround myself with people like that. How do you do that when it's your family? You have a few options.

FIRST, let me just say that simply because you're related by blood (or adoption), doesn't mean that you must continue a relationship with this person. You don't somehow owe them access to your life. You are well within your rights to end any relationship that you see fit to end, and if it's for your mental and emotional health, do what you need to do. That being said, forgiveness will help you make a decision about the relationship without heightened emotions getting in the way. I am estranged from my birth mother (my choice), but if she changed her mind about keeping me a secret, I would certainly explore a relationship with her again. For my sanity though, as long as she is determined to keep my existence a secret, we will need to remain estranged. It's too painful for me, and I choose to protect my children from the same pain. I don't consider the relationship over; I just think of it as paused. It's perfectly okay to create safe boundaries for yourself, and it's very important to maintain them even when someone pushes against them.

ONE OF THE reasons I struggled for most of my life with creating boundaries is that I was terrified that the other person wouldn't like me anymore. It feels silly to write out now, but it was true for so long. I thought that if I said, "Hey, I love you so much, but I need a little more time in-between visits instead of seeing you five times a week," then the person would be devastated, and our friendship would end. The fact is a good friend/family member will understand your boundaries or at the very least respect them.

. . .

WHEN SOMEONE IS SPEAKING death over you (insults, slanders, put-downs, discouragement, etc.), I like to say these four magic words out loud, "I don't receive that." It's simple and effective, and here's why: Humans are easy to program. This is why we remember TV-commercial jingles we haven't heard in twenty years. Someone (especially family members when we're children) speaks something over us, and we either consciously agree with it or don't reject it, and then the slur or opinion buries itself into our subconscious. Have you ever seen the movie *Inception*? It's absolutely brilliant because it illustrates the labyrinth caused by repressed memories in the unconscious mind. This is basically what happens to us when we receive the garbage that's being spoken over us. We find ourselves years later wondering why we keep reliving the same patterns over and over again, and it's because we received what someone said to us and are now living it out.

When you say, "I don't receive that," your conscious mind rejects the words like a forcefield. It also has the added benefit of making people think twice about what they just said to you. I've said those words to many flippant comments about things, like what I can expect with my kids in the future (*just wait until they're teenagers*), my marriage (*the honeymoon phase won't last, you won't always be like this*), my career choices (*most writers never make money selling their books*), going through cancer (*you're probably going to puke every day*), etc. I don't believe these people were trying to be malicious; however, that doesn't mean that I have to receive their experiential truths over my life. Just because that was true for them, doesn't mean it will be true for me. I get to create my own reality, thank you very much, and I choose to only receive the good things people have to say.

Sure, saying those words out loud has gotten me many strange looks, but guess what? The amount of death that's spoken over me has decreased significantly, and whether it's from people actually being more mindful of their words or just not wanting to hear me say this sentence, either way I'll take it.

FINDING PEACE AND MOVING FORWARD

*T*he most important thing I can teach you about finding peace is that you won't ever find it in someone else. Growing up as an adoptee I thought that once I met my birth parents I would suddenly feel whole, and all would be well in the world. I met my birth mother first, and that didn't come with peace. I searched for my birth father many years later, and though the experience was much more positive than the former, I was surprised by how little peace I felt. I wasn't in the dark about my family line anymore, but I still felt fractured.

It was then that I realized how much I had been depending on other people to make me feel whole. Finding wholeness from others is simply not possible and you will only find disappointment where you expected to find completeness. I found my wholeness in Jesus and myself. Once I began to reclaim my voice and step into the person I knew I was always created to be, I began to see everything through a new filter. I was no longer the victim; I was the victor. I was no longer silencing myself to appease others; I was pushing the boundaries and refusing to walk on eggshells. That doesn't mean that I became rude or uncaring about the feelings of others. It simply means that I permitted myself to have my own voice and to express it even when others told me not to.

I HAVE FOUND that the simplest way to find peace is to accept the fact that you can't control anyone else. People will do what they want, and you get to decide how to respond to their actions. A wise woman once told me it's never our circumstances that determine our success in life; it's how we deal with the circumstances that determine our success. People are going to hurt us — that's just a fact of life. When we can get to a place where we forgive immediately without letting the wound fester, create safe boundaries for ourselves, reclaim the voice that trauma may have stolen from us, and step into the power we were always meant to have, that's when peace comes.

That peace will be tested, of course, and the tests may make you wonder if you've truly moved on or not. That's just a part of life! The trick is to remind yourself of who you are and what you stand for. If you aren't exactly sure who that is, spend time figuring it out because it's extremely important. When you know who you are then you will know who you are not, and you will begin to set a boundary fence around yourself to protect that with all you've got.

LEAVE the past where it belongs by choosing forgiveness and freedom for yourself. Some people don't deserve to be forgiven, but you deserve to be free. If you get nothing else out of this book, please just remember that forgiveness is for YOU. It's not about whether the other person has apologized or deserves your forgiveness. It's about freeing yourself from the burden of pain that you've been carrying for far too long. That burden is so heavy that it weighs you down without you even realizing it. Let it go and give yourself time to adjust to the new heights you'll reach without it. You were meant to soar!

Come fly with me, friend.

ALSO BY MEGGAN LARSON

The Truth About Forgiveness Workbook

The Truth About Success (An Anthology)

The Truth About Finding Joy in the Darkness (An
Anthology)

Adopted (Book 1 in the Adopted Trilogy)

Fractured (Book 2 in the Adopted Trilogy)

Reclaimed (Book 3 in the Adopted Trilogy)

Being & Belonging (An Anthology)

Starfish Stories An Anthology Volume 1

ACKNOWLEDGMENTS

Thank you Jesus for showing me everything I know about forgiveness. Rob, thank you for encouraging me in every possible way. I've been in love with you since I was fifteen and that will never change. Kids, you are amazing humans and I love that I get to be your mom. Lauren, thank you for teaching me the truth about boundaries. Lydia, Heather, & Nicole thank you for taking the time to proof-read this book. C.B. Moore, you are the best editor on the planet and I'm so glad I found you. Sharon, thank you answering my millions of questions. To everyone who buys this book, thank you from the bottom of my heart for your amazing support.

xo Meggan

ABOUT THE AUTHOR

Meggan Larson is an award winning author (best selling on Amazon), course creator, wife, mom, and adoptee. She currently lives in Ottawa, Canada with her husband and three children. Through her indie publishing company, Starfish Stories Publishing, she helps the girl who reads all the books become the woman who writes and publishes them.

She lives her life around the concept of the starfish story, where a woman is tossing washed up starfish back into the ocean as they lay dying on the shore, and someone comes along and scoffs at her. He tells her she can't possibly make a difference because there are thousands and she'll never get to them all in time. She picks one up, tosses it back into the water, and says,

"It made a difference to that one."

Meggan wants to make a difference, even if it's just for one person.

Connect with her at hello@megganlarson.com or at her website at https://megganlarson.ca

Made in the USA
Columbia, SC
25 January 2025

52536346R00039